Tiger Salamander Care Handbook:

General Guide on Tiger Salamanders Fostering; Conduct, Health Issues, What They Eat, Lodging & Picking One as a Pet, Etc.

By

Mitchell T. Cudmore

TABLE OF CONTENTS

CHAPTER 1

INTRODUCTION

Tiger salamanders are strikingly lovely creatures that are mainstream outlandish pets. They have a genuinely long life expectancy and as a rule become very agreeable.

Local to North America, these creatures of land and water are found in forests, just as in verdant fields, living in underground tunnels close to waterways. The fundamental shading of tiger salamanders is yellow blotches, spots, or bars against a dark foundation, however the examples and force of shading fluctuate among the subspecies. In addition, they have enormous eyes, short noses, thick necks, solid legs, and long tails. As pets, they can be very vivacious and engaging, adjusting admirably to bondage under the correct conditions. When you have their lodging set up, the consideration is genuinely direct. Hope to invest energy every week on feedings, cleaning, and observing the dampness and temperature.

Species Overview

Basic Name: Tiger lizard, eastern tiger lizard/salamander

Logical Name: Ambystoma tigrinum

Grown-up Size: 6 to 8 inches

Future: 10 to 15 years

Colour:

Grey

Yellow

Brown

Black

Green

Type of Skin:

Permeable

CHAPTER 2

TIGER SALAMANDER CONDUCT, LODGING & OTHER SALIENT INFORMATION

Tiger Salamander Conduct

In contrast to numerous different lizards, tiger salamanders are regularly amicable and tough pets. On schedule, most tiger salamanders will conquer any dread of people. What's more, rather they regularly will follow their attendants' development from inside their nook, just as reach toward hands offering food. Notwithstanding, they ought to be manoeuvred carefully because of their fragile skin. They're not typically forceful and can be kept with another lizard; however they needn't bother with the organization. In any case, it ought to be noticed that they have been known to devour other tiger salamanders, particularly when there is an absence of food.

Lodging the Tiger Salamander

The larval stage is completely sea-going, so these tiger lizards can live in an aquarium with 6 creeps of water and a few rocks to stow away in. They ought to be kept somewhere in the range of 65 and 70 degrees Fahrenheit (18 to 21 degrees Celsius) and not surpassing 72 degrees Fahrenheit (22 degrees Celsius). A decent water channel is required, and air circulation with an air stone is ideal. Give specific consideration to the water quality, particularly smelling

salts development and the water pH.
After months to years, the hatchling will lose its gills and rise up out of the water to take on its grown-up structure. As this happens, bit by bit decrease the measure of water in the tank, and give a land region. When transformation is finished, the salamander can be kept in an earthly tank arrangement. A 10-gallon tank at least with a firmly fitting cover that permits wind current. One end ought to have water while the

opposite end ought to be a raised dry territory. When cleaning the tank, just utilize heated water and no cleansers. Spot clean the tank day by day for excrement or uneaten food and dispose them off. What's more, plan to do a full cleaning of the whole climate generally at regular intervals. Again, a large portion of the sorts of salamander incline toward cool, soggy environmental factors. Nonetheless, they are relentless creatures. Consequently, keeping up ideal temperatures is vital for their wellbeing. In the event that you are keeping tiger salamander in your home, the temperature of the terrarium ought to be kept up between 65 – 70 °F. For fire lizards, the temperature ought to never cross 68 °F.

The walled area for this creature should be clammy, yet not wet. For tiger salamanders and fire lizards, which are the most well-known assortments available to be purchased in the US, sphagnum greenery, bark chippings, or preparing fertilizer will make great substrate. Guarantee that the terrariums for the tiger or fire lizards have concealing spots. Additionally remember a dish of water for the nook and fog the tank consistently. You need to guarantee that the

tank isn't wet, as they are inclined to contaminations brought about by microscopic organisms and parasite.
On the off chance that you need to keep a normal measured pair of one or the other animal categories, the tank ought to be at 24×16×18 inches (60×40×45 cm) huge. This really differs as per the size of the species. Ensure that the terrarium has a protected top, as lizards or salamanders are eminent slick creatures. You need to keep up moistness in the terrarium

and simultaneously, look out for development of shape in the tank.

Tigersalamanders have a decent craving. They additionally discharge a decent sum squander material. Thusly, the tank should be cleaned consistently. Alongside seeing to the prerequisite of stickiness, guarantee that the tank has great ventilation so the climate in the fenced area doesn't get foul.

Warmth

Warming is normally not needed, as tiger salamanders ought to be kept at around 50 to 75 degrees Fahrenheit (10 to 24 degrees Celsius). Temperatures over 80 degrees Fahrenheit (27 degrees Celsius) can pressure or hurt a tiger salamander.

Light

UV lighting isn't needed, yet a standard day-night pattern of around 12 hours of light and 12 hours of murkiness each day ought to be kept up.

Utilize radiant lighting, ideally on a clock.

Dampness

Tiger salamanders are inclined toward a stickiness level of around 70%. Keep up this through standard moistening, water, and live plants inside the tank. Utilize a hygrometer to screen the moistness.

Substrate

Substrate is the material utilized on the lower part of your pet's walled area. In addition to the fact that it helps to mirror a common habitat, yet it additionally builds stickiness and permits the creature to fulfil its tunnelling nature. Give a substrate in any event 4 inches that is appropriate for tunnelling. Anything that keeps up some dampness and is delicate on a lizard's skin is fine. Numerous proprietors use fertilized soil (with no vermiculite or synthetic compounds), coconut husk, or sphagnum greenery. Rock isn't suitable, as it's excessively harsh and doesn't remain damp. Likewise, give plants, bark pieces, smooth rocks, and other natural materials as concealing spots.

CHAPTER 3

TIGER SALAMANDER DIET, AILMENTS & PICKING ONE FOR YOURSELF

Food as Well as Water

Tiger salamanders have a sound hunger. Be that as it

may, they ought not to be overloaded, as they will get corpulent. The hatchling eats oceanic spineless creatures, for example, brackish water shrimp, creepy crawlies, little fish, and worms. Grown-ups eat a choice of feeder creepy crawlies, like crickets, worms, and wax worms. You can likewise take care of them with a periodic pinkie mouse and wild-got bugs, insofar as you're certain they're from a space that is liberated from pesticides and different synthetics. Taking care of them should happen one to three times each week to keep a solid body weight. Your veterinarian ought to exhort you on how much and how regularly to take care of your creature, as it can differ dependent on size and age.

In the event that your tank doesn't as of now have a water region, a huge dish of de-chlorinated water ought to be given to grown-up salamanders. Ensure it's close to 1 to 2 inches down. Your salamander may appreciate absorbing the dish, so the water will require normal cleaning.

Regular Health Plus Behaviour Problems

Tiger salamanders are helpless to respiratory contaminations, with manifestations including wheezing and bodily fluid around the nose and mouth. This frequently results from inappropriate temperatures or dampness levels in their current circumstance. Parasitic contaminations additionally are fairly regular in tiger salamander, particularly if their resistant framework is as of now battling another issue. On the off chance that your tiger salamander appears to be drowsy or is getting thinner, these are indication of a debilitated creature; carry it to a veterinarian who represents considerable authority in outlandish pets.

Picking Your Amazing Tiger Salamander

Similarly as with most intriguing pets, it's a poorly conceived notion to attempt to keep a wild salamander in bondage. For one, it very well may be illicit to take a salamander from the wild where you reside. Also, wild creatures regularly neglect to flourish in imprisonment. All things considered, track down a respectable raiser or salvage association. However, realize that hostage reproduced tiger salamander are not generally accessible in light of the fact that rearing has demonstrated troublesome. The merchant ought to have the option to give some knowledge about the creature's wellbeing, beginning, and character. Hope to pay around $50.

When in doubt, try not to buy any salamander with dry patches on its skin, as this can demonstrate an issue with shedding. Also, search for indications of a respiratory contamination, particularly overabundance bodily fluid. A sound tiger salamander's eyes ought to be clear and liberated from any discharge, and it should take food promptly when it's advertised.

CHAPTER4

FURTHER FACTS ABOUT TIGER SALAMANDERS & THEIR NOTABLE THREATS

The tiger salamander has a fairly short, adjusted nose, solid legs, a thick head, and a long tail. The specific tones and examples change all through the whole reach dependent on the species, yet the base shade of the body is generally earthy coloured, green, or dim. This is overlaid with dazzling yellow or blunter earthy coloured spots or stripes, which offer it to the name. In the same way as other different sorts of salamander, this species can recover a separated appendage. These appendages at times have an unexpected pigmentation in comparison to the remainder of the body.

The tiger salamander has permeable skin through which it relaxes. It additionally should continually emit bodily fluid to keep the skin wet. Sadly, this permeable skin additionally leaves it exceptionally defenceless against contamination.

The eastern tiger salamander is the authority state land and water proficient of Illinois.

Tiger Salamander Predators as well as their Threats

The tiger salamanders faces numerous dangers in the wild, including predation, contamination, deforestation and natural surroundings obliteration, high corrosiveness levels in their rearing pools, and surprisingly vehicular mishaps. Corrosive downpour was a specific issue before the execution of the Clean Air Act of 1990, which, as per the National Geographic, cut sulfur dioxide outflows by 88% starting at 2017. Nitrogen dioxide levels additionally fell by half in a similar period.

What eats the tiger salamander?

A grown-up tiger lizard is gone after by birds (like owls), turtles, snakes, badgers, and wildcats. The hatchlings are likewise defenceless against oceanic creepy crawlies and snakes.

Tiger Salamander Reproduction, Babies, and Lifespan

The tiger salamander starts the regenerative interaction eventually between pre-spring and late-winter when they relocate to their aggregate rearing pools. The romance interaction includes a convoluted arrangement of practices. After the male tracks down a reasonable mate, he will poke her with his head to communicate his advantage. She responds this conduct by bumping the male's vent territory, actuating him to deliver his sperm material, which the female will then gather. The opposition for females is wild to such an extent that a few guys will intrude on the romance cycle of another male and endeavour to substitute his own sperm all things being equal.

After a short incubation time of just a couple of days, the female lays up to 100 eggs all at once and afterward ties down them to twigs, grasses, and leaves at the lower part of the pool. She can store numerous masses of eggs in a solitary rearing season to guarantee the reasonability of the future. A large number of these youthful are not expected to endure, and the guardians give no specific assurance to them. The generation methodology depends on sheer numbers.

After a brooding time of around a month, the hatchlings rise out of the eggs with a yellowish or olive body, dim blotches or stripes at the edge, a white gut, enormous outside gills, and an amphibian tail. They burn through the vast majority of the spring and late-spring period taking care of and filling in the first pool of their introduction to the world. At around two to five months old enough, they go through a groundbreaking transformation by which they arrive at their grown-up stage. As they adjust to another earthbound life, the lizards completely lose their gills and foster a bunch of lungs to relax.

Assuming conditions ashore are especially poor, the hatchling may defer in transformation however long important so they can keep on living submerged. In spite of the fact that they are as yet ready to explicitly recreate, these creatures keep up a similar fundamental physiology as their larval stage through a cycle known as neoteny. The creature can be stuck in the larval structure for quite a long time, a long time, or even their whole lives. Be that as it may, they actually hold the alternative to go through transformation whenever the conditions improve.

In the event that they endure the adolescent stage, when a large number of them succumb to hunters, the normal salamander arrives at sexual development at around four to five years old. This species has a life expectancy of 10 to 16 years in the wild – moderately enduring for a lizard. A few of them have been known to live very nearly 25 years in bondage.

Tiger Salamander Population

These creatures are as of now viewed as types of least worry by the IUCN Red List. It isn't exactly known the number of these lizards that exist in the wild, yet populace numbers give off an impression of being steady, notwithstanding a few populaces being secluded and divided from one another. The decay of contamination, corrosive downpour, and environment obliteration has assisted with getting the fate of this species.

Are tiger salamanders acceptable pets?

In case you're willing to commit the time and thoughtfulness regarding its appropriate consideration, at that point the tiger salamanders can flourish in bondage. It is among the more mainstream colourful pets as a result of its nice character; it moderately has long life expectancy and interesting conduct too. Given sufficient opportunity, it should get used to its proprietor and even react decidedly to your essence. Be that as it may, because of the touchy skin, you ought to be cautious about dealing with this animal.

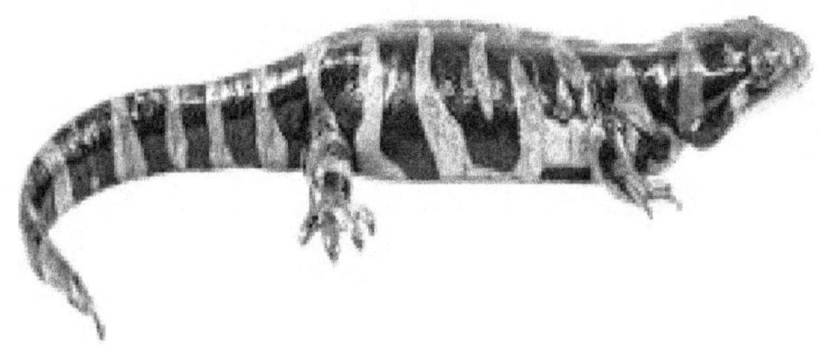

CHAPTER 5

SALAMANDER FUN & AMAZING TIPS

Fun Tips for You

Salamanders don't have break zones in their tails as certain reptiles do, yet can recover whole appendages. Recovered parts are normally recognizable by the absence of trademark pigmentation.

On the off chance that they have lungs, as the tiger salamander does, they siphon air in and out by gular siphoning (bringing down and raising the floor of the mouth).

Commonly, tiger salamander hatchlings take care of and

develop throughout the spring and late-spring and transform 2 to 5 months subsequent to incubating. Be that as it may, a few populaces won't ever transform. In regions where the conditions encompassing perpetual lakes are dry and unwelcoming, they may hold certain larval attributes that permit them to live submerged. These creatures develop in the water and can duplicate, however they keep up the body of a juvenile salamander – a marvel called neoteny. Should natural conditions improve, they may transform into an earthbound grown-up.

Biology and Conservation

These huge lizards are dinners for some creatures like snakes, turtles, birds, and fish. They may originate before on creepy crawlies, worms, little vertebrates, and surprisingly different creatures of land and water.

Creatures of land and water have permeable skin and react rapidly to changes in the climate. The strength of their populaces can be a pointer of the wellbeing of the climate.

Ongoing reviews have recognized about just 90 tiger salamanders rearing lakes in New York. Its status at these excess locales is shaky due to pesticides and different impurities, danger of advancement, and other land use designs. Lake

aggravation, ruthless fish presentation, and extending bullfrog populaces undermine yearly multiplication.
Expanded street development has likewise isolated the living space, endangering relocating grown-ups

CHAPTER 6

CONCLUSION

Having gone through the nitty-gritty of tiger salamanders; I am sure you will stick to the guidelines of caring/ nurturing your amazing salamanders.

Remember, there no shot-cuts to caring for your new pet (TIGER SALAMANDERS).

All the best to you!

THE END.

www.ingramcontent.com/pod-product-compliance
Ingram Content Group UK Ltd.
Pitfield, Milton Keynes, MK11 3LW, UK
UKHW021934190726
13853UKWH00004B/1434

9 798507 256914